Finding Light

Clare Matanle

Hope Cottage Publications

Published by:
Hope Cottage Publications
Willand, Devon, UK
Supporting Headcase Cancer Trust. www.headcase.org.uk

Email: clarematanle@btinternet.com

First published in 2018

Cover design by Streamline Photography & Design
Candle image throughout book © Kim Hicks

ISBN: 978-1-9999958-0-5

British Library Cataloguing-in-Publication Data
A catalogue record for this book is available from the British Library.

Typeset by Streamline Photography & Design, Uffculme, Devon.
Printed and bound by Biddles Books Limited.

Front cover image: © Adobe Stock
Back cover image: © Adobe Stock

Finding Light

"Finding Light"
is a gathering together of my thoughts,
discovered in the ashes, in the maze and along my path through
times of intense darkness.

There have been moments of sudden illumination
and others when the light has
dawned gradually.
Light has been found in many different ways.

"Finding Light"
is an offering of my candle
to fellow travellers along the way.

Contents

1 Paths

Paths converge on the West Wales sand,
17, love in the moonlight,
Our time began as we studied the land,
Marloes, Wooltack, Dale.

His heartbeat, heard through Aran wool,
Amidst primroses and bluebells,
Woodland meanderings above river, full,
Calstock, Cotehele, Tamar.

Camouflaged, trudging through bracken and bog,
Striding across the heather,
Map and compass, tors in the fog,
Dartmoor, Pen-y-Fan, Brecon.

Parka coats zipped against the storm,
Kisses through the raindrops,
Leaning together, keeping warm,
Wight, Portland, Plymouth.

Footpaths followed to the sea,
Love pledged beside the beach huts,
Hearts linked together, him to me,
Hordle, Taddiford, Barton,

In tandem, exploring the forest tracks,
Pedalling on together,
All that we needed packed on our backs,
Setthorns, Longslade, Denny.

The way to work, beside the stream,
Cycling under the railway,
Racing back home together to dream,
Willowdene, Pinewood, Ashley.

The world seen through our children's eyes,
Wandering at their pace,
Discoveries adorned with their surprise,
Puddle, Pebble, Twig.

Along darker paths, confusing ways,
Navigating together,
A light still leads us through the haze,
Grief, Depression, Cancer.

Our paths diverge, he's gone on ahead,
Into the sunlit meadow.
The longer track is the way I'm led,
Via Devon, to rejoin in Heaven.

2 What Kind of Love is This?

What kind of love is this?
> *- That lives in sunshine, dies in rain,*
> *- That turns its back and walks away.*

What kind of love is this?
> *- That walks beside on the winding pathway,*
> *- That chooses to stay when the storm clouds loom.*

What kind of love is this?
> *- That sticks together in mud-filled trenches,*
> *- That wades the river, hand in hand.*

What kind of love is this?
> *- That builds a bridge across the swampland,*
> *- That sees the rainbow in the rain.*

What kind of love is this?
>*— That sweeps, uplifts with a surf-wave power,*
>*— That leaves memory-prints in the soft seashore.*

What kind of love is this?
>*— That rests content in sun-filled meadows,*
>*— That spreads a "kitten-chasing-butterflies" joy.*

What kind of love is this?
>*— That gives and lifts, cares, cries and laughs,*
>*— That bonds two lives together as one.*

What kind of love is this?
>*— That knows each love-created heartbeat,*
>*— That loved before life and is forever Love.*

3 Sitting in the Ashes

I saw her, slumped, in the ash on the hearth,
Her wedding dress smeared and singed.
Each piece of her home was shrouded in dust,
Her door lay shattered, unhinged.

The lightning strike that blew off the roof,
Shot through her, leaving her stunned.
She sat there, dazed, body bruised and sore,
Any speech or touch she shunned.

Her home fell apart, as if hit by a bomb,
Blown away by a sudden fierce storm.
The fire, once the heart of the home, went out,
She was bereft in the cold light of dawn.

I'll sit here, beside her, we won't have to speak,
The choice of words is hers.
And if, perhaps, she wants to get up,
I'll give her my hand when she stirs.

4 p.s.

The Post Script,
               the after word,
written after the Pivotal Second
when his last
            heartbeat
                  was heard.
Profound Silence,
        Peace Settles.

The Preliminary Situation,
        his funeral
               to be arranged.
People Surround,
        Provide Support,
hold me together, I'm not deranged.
People Strengthen,
        Peace Soothes.

Purpose Shattered,
>   what to do now?
Our life dismantled, Packing Starts,
My home surrendered,
>   a new beginning,

>   somehow?
A Place Secured,
>   Peace Shelters.

Past Shadows
>   show Painful Scars

>   in sharp relief.
Peace Seeps away in the widow's maze.
Periscope Sight
>   offers Personal Solutions

>   to my grief.
Peaceful Solace,
>   Post Steve.

5 | Soliloquy

*...and the story continued with half
the words missing
in embers grown dim where the
firelight once burned
and visions, bejewelled with the
mistings of dreaming,
formed web threads that trailed as
the blank pages turned.*

6 *My Beating Heart*

Listening in the night time shadows,
Lonely beating of my heart.
Pulsing onward through the darkness,
Through the storm without a chart.

Pounding with a lava anger,
Burning hot, cold sweat on brow.
Fluttering with fearful thinking,
Why? and When? What if? What now?

All around the tempest rages,
Tearing trees and earth apart.
Mirroring the storm within me,
"Help me, please and save my heart!"

One single word, as light is dawning,
Settles on my troubled mind.
"Solace", given like a blanket,
Meaning? This I have to find.

"Solace" from the Loving Father,
Wrapping me, held in His arm.
Bathing me with consolation,
Comfort, help, no fear of harm.

With every beat my heart says "Thank you,"
Loving Father, for your care.
Through life's storms you never leave me,
Always loving, always there.

God, whose heart beats beyond endings,
Through the whirlwind and the hail,
Match my heartbeat to your tempo,
God, whose love will never fail.

7 Nobody Knows

Nobody can be me,
This I'm beginning to see.
Someone else I may seek,
But I am quite unique,
Nobody else can be me.

Nobody lives my life,
The good, the bad and the strife.
How I live, I don't show,
No one else can know,
Nobody else lives my life.

Nobody knows my thoughts,
All the shoulds and the coulds and the oughts,
All the things that I find
In the maze of my mind,
Nobody else knows my thoughts.

Nobody gives me grief,
I can choose between hurt and relief.
When my past is revealed
My deep wounds can be healed,
Nobody else gives me grief.

Nobody chooses my way,
I can choose what I'm going to say.
I can choose left or right,
Choose to walk in the Light,
Nobody else chooses my way.

Nobody walks beside,
Unless invited for the ride.
Trusted people who stay
Up and down – all the way,
Nobody else walks beside.

Nobody knows the real me,
Except the One who can see
Right into my soul,
Formed each part of the whole,
Nobody else knows me.

8 Descendants of the Wolf

A wail in the night! I awake with a start!
What is it that stirs up such fear?
On the edge of awareness, way off in the woods,
it's the howl of the wolf that I hear.

A primitive sound, as it bays at the moon, sends shivers up my spine!
I'm transported back to my ancestral home.
The cave and the wagon are mine.
And Fear was real – he led a fierce pack of wolves that roamed through the night,
Encircling any that ventured alone,
keeping others corralled by fright.

Through the passage of time, the wolf has been tamed
and bred for domestication.
The basic traits of primitive Fear,
morphed by diversification.
But the wolf within lies just under the skin
of the lapdog, the hound and Alsatian.
Left unchecked, unrestrained, they revert to the wild,
overriding their modern mutation.

Many crippling fears dog our footsteps today, we fear for our lives in our mind.
We need a safe place as the pack runs amok
and a guard on the door we must find.
Whatever the fears, even those held for years, however complicated,
When restrained and retrained and no longer in charge,
they're subdued and moderated.

And, if wolves start to howl in the dead of the night,
clawing, slinking their way inside,
The one who is Alpha frees the prisoner within,
throwing Fear and the pack outside!

9 Pendulum

The pendulum swings,
Alarm bells ring,
What Quasimodo hangs on the rope?
Who rattled my chain, setting dogs barking?
Who pressed the button, exploding my brain?

Don't ask that question or demand of me!
Ringing in my ears!
Head-banging cacophony!

I don't care anymore!
Don't go there!
I've cared and lost too much!

The big boys wound my swing up,
over-swung it, over the top bar.
Can someone help me unwind it?

Chains rattle,

It falls,

Jangling swerves

become curves,
inviting me to swing again.

Swing away to a place of safety,
into the comfort zone.
Say No!   Stay here!   You're OK,   Rest.

Refusing to go beyond my extremities,
to shatter the stay and break the bell,
I'll choose my own course,   considered,   measured,
equilibrium sought,
erratic swings smoothed,
a gentle chiming.

10   *Just A **Little Bit Stressed***

I've not been the one to need the aid of a Travel Kalm or a Kwell,
But today, in the rush of a pre-dawn start,
I'm feeling quite unwell.
I feel sick!

I'll try looking out, take a wider view of the scene, – that's a good decision.
But my focus is blurred by a thick worry-fog,
All I see is in tunnel-vision.
I can't see!

I'll do some deep breathing, – I know that technique, I've counted as others have heaved.
I'll shut my eyes, pretend I'm asleep,
Count and gasp till I feel relieved.
I will count!

I've read the book, know it all, done the course, – "Understanding Anxiety",
But nothing's prepared me for what it is like
When the person afflicted is me.
It is me!

I've always been calm in a crisis before, they say that I look so serene,
I've been there beside those who rant their despair,
But this isn't me watching the scene.
This is me!

Stop-the-coach! Let-me-off! I need some fresh air! I'm boiling! I need to feel colder!
Is the air-con on? I can't feel the breeze!
Just leave me on the hard-shoulder!
I-can't-breathe!

Please just talk to me – I don't care what about! Just fill my head with your chatter,
So I don't have to think of how small this space is
And you don't have to ask, "What's the matter?"
It's just me!

The adrenaline spike will subside in a while, so I've read – it's a "Panic Attack".
If my heart keeps on beating and I can still breathe,
I'll survive the journey back.
I'm still alive...... at the moment!

11 | The Wall

Mizzle-Muddled Addle-Faddled
Skiddle-Skaddle Cricky-crack
Skirl-Screamer Craze-curling
Off the Wall and back

Grief-ghettoed Dire-dreamer
Hurt-heaving Spittle-Spat
Mire-Mazed Empty-eyeing
To the Wall Just Sat

Undayed Sun-Shunner
Door-ajarring Rat-A-Tat
Wretch-reacher Finger-tipping
Through the Wall Who's that?

12 Sparkly Hammock Moments

Amidst life's hectic whirl-around
I hope that you will find
Sparkly Hammock Moments
For your body, soul and mind.

A resting place for tired limbs
When strength has ebbed away.
"I give up, Lord – over to you,"
Is all that we can say.

Climb into your hammock,
Exhausted by your fears.
Resting in the rainbows
As God's love shines through your tears.

A rainbow through the lashing rain
When feelings have been torn.
Your spirit lifted by the Lord
who comforts those forlorn.

Resting in your "hammock,"
Your "life-boat" or your bed –
God gives a place that's right for you,
With "duvet" over head.

A "duvet" of His comfort,
His solace and His peace.
Soothing every tension,
When all our strivings cease.

A long and wearing illness
Becomes a journey too.
While resting in your hammock,
God clears the road for you.

Sparkly Hammock Moments
Aren't time-sensitive you'll find.
A flash of revelation
Can refresh a weary mind.

The beauty of the world around
Can strengthen our belief.
God's vibrant life in everything,
Unfurling every leaf.

Look for your Sparkly Hammock
As you travel life's highway.
Detour, find rest and be refreshed,
In God's hand – gently sway.

13 PULL YOUR SOCKS UP!

"PULL YOUR SOCKS UP!
STRAIGHTEN YOUR TIE!
HEAD UP, STAND TALL, SHOULDERS BACK!
STAND TO ATTENTION!
PAY ATTENTION!
A SPINE IS WHAT YOU LACK!

STOP YOUR COMPLAINING!
JUST LOOK AROUND,
MANY ARE WORSE OFF THAN YOU!
MAKE SOME NEW FRIENDS,
JOIN SOMETHING! PARTY!
THERE'S SO MUCH THAT YOU COULD DO!"

SHUT UP! PUSH OFF!
You critical voice!
Can't you see I am doing my best!
With depleted resources,
I'm so exhausted!
Cut me some slack! Let me rest!

I can't pull my socks up,
The elastic has gone!
Been under tension too long!
Frayed and unravelled,
Down round my ankles,
They'll sit there until they pong!

When I feel ready,
I'll venture forth,
To the village or the town,
To purchase elastic,
To keep my socks up,
OR I COULD JUST LEAVE THEM DOWN!!

14 Duvet View

Pictures within the grain of wood
Upon the wardrobe door,
Speak a truth to me of my life as it's been,
Which I've never seen before.

Not noticing bunting festooning the room,
My view is confined to the bed.
The spiders, unhindered for months, make their lace,
Matching cobwebs inside my head.

The TV's on stand-by to entertain,
But the screen stays a blank, empty square.
The button's not pressed so the world can't rush in,
I'm safe from the trauma out there.

Discovering stories from so many lives
Inside books in a pile on the floor,
Some solace is found when I find a match
To my own that feels so sore.

Linking through words to a million minds,
Into each unique life I can peek.
An aspect of theirs may mirror mine,
"You're not alone", they softly speak.

The library books need to be exchanged.
Why can't I get out of the door?
It takes all day to face the world,
I manage at half past four.

They say, "A body has to eat",
Simple food would meet the need.
At the checkout, tears fall at a kindly word,
I beat a retreat with all speed.

Back in my bedroom, exhausted, I rest,
The grey world outside kept at bay.
The spiders' eviction can wait until spring,
It's Wonder Woman's duvet day.

15 I'm Tired of Being a Banker

I'm tired of being a "banker", the engine that helps up the hill.
When the train is heavy, the wheels start to slip
And it comes to a sudden standstill.

A banker is needed to assist if a loco cannot cope.
Working together, combining their power,
The train is hauled up the slope.

For years, I've been the banker, the one who helps when it's tough.
I've been there for others who've run out of steam,
But now I've just had enough!

I want to divert to a branch line and run on a different track.
Take the slow train down to the market town
And then gently trundle back.

16   Little Voice

A whisper in my heart,
What do I really want to do?
Not should, ought or have to.

My little voice has been drowned out by stronger voices.
The demands of life, shouting for attention.
Responsibilities
Working
Caring
Crises.

Now is the time to listen to my little voice,
Tentatively speaking,
Expecting to be drowned out again,
Shouted down again.

A still small voice,
Is that God or me?

A still, small voice of calm,
Speaking through earthquake, wind and fire,
Guiding, giving me my heart's desire,

Giving me permission
To listen
To the whisperings
Of my little voice.

17 Decisions, Decisions

"Well done!" "Way to go!" Thanks, but I'm not too sure!
Is that the right decision?
What if I choose to go that way?
Will my friends be filled with derision?

Influenced strongly by what people think,
I want help to know what to do,
But in the end I have to decide,
It's up to me to work things through.

I stand at a crossroad, peer this way and that,
Stopped, stymied and silenced by fear.
Shall I choose that route or take this path?
The right way is hidden, unclear.

If I'd only said "Yes" and not "No" at that point,
Headed off down that road, been insistent,
I would not be here, regretting the past,
That different life's non-existent.

No good comes from longing for what never has been,
Regret wrecks the present, somehow.
The past can't be changed, whatever we try,
We can only influence the now.

So what do I want at this moment in time?
Which way sits right within?
If I weigh pros and cons, bravely choose a path,
The next leg of my life can begin.

18 *Woolly*

Discarded dags of the mind
Snagged on the barbs of a memory.

Washed in hot tears of pain.

Tangled thoughts unravelled,
Laid out, bleaching on a sun-lit thorn hedge.

Pulled apart, combed, carded – impurities released,
The past raked up, brought to the surface.

Dyed in the wool, clouded, black and white thinking,
Seen in a different light,
Transformed, both subtle and vivid.

Thinking coloured by a myriad of choices,
A kaleidoscope of possibilities.

Thought-threads aligned, spun together
New-formed strength of mind,
Twined for a purpose.

19 Let It Go!

No More Stiff upper Lip! I'M Letting it Slip!
No More Headaches FroM Holding the TeNsioN!
I'M Letting it go! Letting all the tears FLoW,
About things I've Not dared to MeNtioN!

I've Kept it all iN, I'd just bear it and griN,
"I'M FiNe thaNKS!" – My Method oF phrasiNg.
I caN Let it all out! I caN ScreaM! I caN SHout!
The reLieF it brings! Quite aMaziNg!

42

I can do as I please! Not worn out on my knees,
I'll send "shoulds" "oughts" and "musts" packing!
Self-compassion, I find, flows down into my mind,
I'm released! A personal Fracking!

20 Best Friends Again

I was rushing around the other day
And met Myself coming back.
There I was, right in front of Me,
Totally on the wrong track.

I gave Myself a talking to,
I said that this wouldn't do!
"Some Me-time is what is needed,
Before we all shoot through!"

I had ignored Myself through busyness,
Not seeing what others could see.
I had to be kind to Myself again,
Understand Myself and love Me.

I had breakfast by Myself today,
For Me – an unusual treat!
I, quite often beside Myself,
Could now listen and talk and meet.

I took time to allow Myself to breathe,
A good move, it seemed to be.
By allowing Myself to come to the fore,
Amazingly, I could be Me!

I said to Myself, "Let's do this again!"
And that really agreed with Me.
"Let's get together very soon!"
"How about for afternoon tea?"

21 Turning Out

A green velvet dress, tearful smiles lace the memory,
Kept in the cupboard, a full quarter century.
Brought into the light, to consider again,
For the charity bag? Or should it remain?

Mum and Dad's Ruby Wedding, – their 40th year,
Friends and family all gathering together to hear,
Their life story told with love, laughter and rhyme,
Keys that opened new doors for them throughout their time.

Laura Ashley, size 12, a deep bottle green,
My double-star colour, how slim I had been.
Chestnut hair piled up, soft tendril on cheek,
Any grey hair appearing, the tweezers would tweak.

My brother beside me, our family, loved ones,
Our parents, their children, our boys – their grandsons.
Good friends from the past gave them such a surprise!
A beautiful memory, the love in their eyes.

Twenty-five years later, three loved ones have left,
As time marches on, I can feel quite bereft.
No longer a daughter or even a wife,
"Orphan" and "widow" are part of my life.

My brother and I are both grandparents now,
Not clones of our parents, time's changed us somehow.
His hair style's the same, though the colour's now lighter,
My tumbling curls are now bobbed, blonde and brighter!

I could return my green dress to the cupboard again,
Shut away in the dark where my memories remain,
Or transform it with stitches, embellish with beads,
Create a design and see where it leads.

Choosing beautiful buttons and Granny's old lace,
With old and new fabric, each having a place,
I'm reminded of many good times in the past,
But now I'll move forward, make new memories that last.

My memories held firmly in fabric and thread,
Highlighted moments from the way I've been led.
Re-purposed green dress, large enough, not too small,
Carries old and new memories,
                              green velvet hold-all.

22 Bird Feeder

Robin came early for breakfast today,
As mist signalled the end of the night,
She took just one seed but then had to flee,
As fierce sparrows swooped in for a fight.

"Come back, little Robin, when the wild flock has gone,
When the garden is quiet and still.
Take your time, there's no hurry, choose what you need,
Eat until you've had your fill."

Flocking together or coming alone,
To the banqueting station to feed,
Sunflower, suet, nyger and nut,
With mixed seed, it meets each bird's need.

Feeling denied of the things that I need,
I'm empty, with nothing to give.
I need to replenish, to be understood,
Receive comfort to know how to live.

I'm searching for crumbs, crawling 'round on the floor,
Not realising that just up above,
Is a table prepared, with all that I need,
A banquet offered with love.

The Host bids me welcome, "Come sit and receive",
I'm more precious than sparrows, I'm told.
The One who knows each fluttering heart,
Opens His arms wide to hold.

Bright sunshine breaks through the dank morning mist,
As I rest, replenished, relieved.
And a robin sings as she takes a seed,
Like me - thankful for all she's received.

23 | Stuff and Stones

The nitty gritty stuff of life that gets into your hair,
Under your feet, under your skin, stuff gets everywhere.
The little stuff, the HUGE stuff that comes into your head,
Stuff that creeps into your home and accumulates under the bed.
Stuff to be done outside our choice, above and beyond all reason.
Stuff that demands our time and strength, in and out of every season.

And God speaks, – *"Come and sit with me."*
"Lord, there's so much stuff to do! There's this and that and him and her,
There is no time for you."
"Come away with me to a peaceful place, – just for a couple of days,
Where there's no stuff to cloud your mind and my path shines through the haze.
I'll show you stuff to be cleared out, forgive, put right, to cease.
Come – rest with me, don't talk, just wait – and I will give you peace."
"Come away and talk with me," – You speak into my heart.
"Yes, Lord, I am coming, – I'll no longer stay apart."

You brought us all from different lives, through storms and fearsome weather,
From north and south and east and west, you brought us all together.
Each one precious to you, Lord, chosen to be there,
Part of your plan before time began, of which we weren't aware.
Each one so very different, unique, a precious gem,
Worshipping together, we reached to touch your hem.

We were the cradled baby, felt love and comfort meet,
Your healing cloak was wrapped around, whilst sitting at your feet.
A sacrifice of praise we gave, to you – our precious Lord,
And you gave back your soothing balm, the oil of gladness poured.
An atmosphere of love and peace, accepting and forgiving,
A place of openness and rest, where broken hearts start living.
You drew us all together as we gazed upon your face,
Short or tall, big or small, jigsaw pieces all in place.

A building work has started, a new thing has begun.
The living stones, together placed, stand side by side as one.
Each stone's been quarried, used and worn, then left just where they fall,
Life's chisel marks so visible, what use are they at all?
But the builder sees, with different eyes, each cherished stone's potential.
He places each and every one, his hand so reverential.
Not scrubbing off the moss or mould, no mud washed off with water,
He uses them just as they are and beds them in with mortar.

A thing of beauty, – every stone adds to the final face,
A solid wall is being built 'round God's new meeting place.
He builds the walls the modern way, combines to make it thick,
With breeze blocks, old foundation stones, glazed uPVC, new bricks.

Father's house is being extended,
The Cornerstone – His Son,
Joined by the Holy Spirit,
Including everyone.

24 Looking for Lollipops

Brown linoleum floor in the echoing hall,
We climbed the steep stairs to meet
The doctor and dentist who administered pain,
I was promised a sweet as a treat.

Now passing a café and hospital shops,
We enter a twilight world,
Of pain and procedures, treatment and tests,
Cake against cancer is hurled.

His is a raspberry white chocolate muffin,
The lemon and poppy seed's mine.
We cling to the normal amidst the abnormal,
A tightrope, a very fine line.

Appointments I keep to open myself,
Lancing the boil within,
Pouring all into empathetic ears,
Understanding what's under my skin.

Then needing to hide in a book or a mag,
There's just the menu to read.
Not seeing clearly the words on the page,
Stare and wait, let the turmoil recede.

The level of upset is measured against
The need for the comfort of food,
And next to the café are beautiful clothes
Just waiting to lift my mood.

Conversations with others reveal common ground,
Tea, talking and cake ease some pains,
But a brown lino place is kept hidden inside,
A hurt child without lollipops remains.

No sweetie or cake can fill the void
Where the silent cries go unheeded,
But compassion we share and give to ourselves
Soothes the pain, brings relief where it's needed.

25 *Praying Hard*

Oh God! Don't let her die!
I can't bear these loved ones to go through the pain that I did!
I've pleaded all night, aware that she might
and my prayers might go unheeded.

But I know that's untrue!
And I always knew that each whisper of mine's not ignored.
But that's not to say, if I follow your way
that I'll get what I want or implored.

But, please God, let her live!
She's got so much to give in her world with her husband and baby.
How will they survive, if she's not alive?
Could your plan let her live? Just maybe?

As we wait to hear,
Our minds muddled with fear, thought processes so erratic,
Her loved ones lives switched from thrive to survive,
their days lived on automatic.

I could fast! Go without!
Would my prayers have more clout if I prayed through the night, shedding tears?
As I plead and shout, the truth comes out,
my prayers are driven by fears.

Dear God, in this life,
There's such suffering and strife! It's part of the human condition.
But you taught us to pray, your love shows us the way,
Links our hearts through prayer and petition.

I'll stop speaking now,
Peace is coming, somehow. I don't need to say one more word.
I'm trusting you to carry us through,
it's the prayer from the heart that is heard.

The prayers that I bring
May not change anything but your answer is not a deception.
Your promise remains, that, throughout all the pains,
You will carry us without exception.

So, I'm asking you,
Please, Dear God, guide us through whatever is coming today.
Please carry her gently and all my loved ones,
Give us all that we need, I pray.

26 Flood Management

A full moon, a spring tide and a gale from the north – together they all conspire.
A perfect storm surges down the coast,
>   an unstoppable force, rising higher.
The barriers breached, the sandbags can't keep the water at bay, in it surges.
Homes submerged, lives destroyed, the flood sweeps in,
>   a living hell soon emerges.
Once the storm surge has passed, the waters recede, retreat in the wake of the tide.
The flood ebbs away, the land has been changed,
>   a different way must be tried.

Land allocated for flooding control may give rise to some consternation,
But fields, sometimes covered with water and mud,
>   protect homes from inundation.
With floodgates and channels and sheltering banks, the water can be directed.
The silt that remains when the waters subside
>   gives results that are quite unexpected.

In set-aside places are those who know how to manage outpouring emotion.
Just as the floodplains, sluice gates and drains
divert surges of river and ocean.
A releasing of tears can water the soul, bringing life to exhausted ground.
With support alongside to help channel the flow,
fresh shoots of new thinking are found.

An artist arrives with paper and pen to capture the negative scene.
Ink-black strokes describe trees drowning, lost in the flood,
where there used to be fields of green.
As days go by and the seasons change, streams flow beneath bridges again,
The artist discovers a flower-filled meadow,
sees rainbows that shine through the rain.
He could not have conceived the change there has been – unbelievable transformation.
From a land engulfed, overwhelmed, submerged
has come life after devastation.

27 Hope Cottage

A little house, a garden small with fields and trees beyond the wall.
Bounded by the old train track that ran down the Vale to the dairy and back.
The valley with its leats and rills, a patchwork view to the Blackdown Hills.
A place of hope, a piece of heaven, new life begun in glorious Devon.

At dawn a deer came stepping through, crossing the field to pastures new.
As amber leaves glow on the cherries, birds feast on the autumn berries.
The honking geese, through wind and hail, arrived to winter in the Vale.
While people round their fires huddled, the land lay cold and muddy-puddled.

The rising light way in the east warms the backs of man and beast.
As morning mists clear with the sun, the growing year has now begun.
Rooks gathered in the ancient oak, nests in mind, they caw and croak.
As grubs emerge the rooks all creep across the field between the sheep.

Gaps in the hedge – spring lambs can pass, trespassing to find new grass.
They wander further from the farm, 'til shepherd calls them back from harm.
A green woodpecker, in his tree, surveyed the scene. What could he see?
Ants emerging in the sun, a buffet waiting – just for one.

The cows, let out from winter sheds, ran and skipped and tossed their heads.
Then cattle cropped the grassy field, put goodness back for future yield.
The cows had left, the field was still, when throbbing noise came up the hill.
Shut the windows! Close the door! The muck was flung, then back for more!

A big red tractor came with plough, turned field to shining furrows now.
Top-dressed with lime and harrowed round, the seed was sown, rich earth it found.
Unseen in soil, what would it be? With rain and sun, the shoots we see.
And maize grew up, so straight and tall, it peeped in over the garden wall.

House Martin swoops across blue sky, catching insects flying high.
Nesting safe under the eaves, raises young, then he leaves.
Some sparrows borrowed Martin's nest, for winter roost it was the best.
As summer comes their chicks all fledge, fluttering down to hide in the hedge.

Some flower-friends, transported too, one hundred miles to pastures new,
In Devon's soil a home they found – pinks, mauves, lime greens and whites abound.
Through the flowers the honey bees roam, then fly beyond the farm to home.
Butterflies bask on buddleia, tall, growing on the red stone wall.

The farmer comes to check his field, hoping for a proper yield.
Some days of sunshine without rain would dry the crop and ripen grain.
Harvest time – the cutters clatter! Before the blades the maize stalks shatter.
A harvest dance in figure of eight, headlights blaze, they're working late.

Tractors with trailers piled high, through the village, trundle by.
Down to the farm and back again, to harvest the crop before the rain.
Across the vale the farmers toil, to clear the fields and till the soil.
The lad arrives to neaten the edge, mows the margin and trims the hedge.

A tractor returns with gleaming plough, furrows the field in readiness now.
Harrowed and sown within the day, the seed is ready to grow away.
Rooks sweep in across the vale, riding on an autumn gale.
Stormy days, to them, don't matter. They soar and swoop or crouch and chatter.

With autumn mists and shorter days, the geese come, calling through the haze.
A new crop greens the field again, lashed by wind and driving rain.
Sparrows busy with dry grass, refurbish nests as cold winds pass.
And through the seasons here, I've found, my own position has turned around.

The year began with haste and worry, — things must be done in such a hurry.
Now's the time to pause and wait, with elbows resting on the gate.
House, garden, wall, field, trees and sky, a year of change has rolled on by.
Hope Cottage, home, retreat, a nest – God's gift to me, my place of rest.

28 Coping

Being real with fellow-grievers, we share thoughts and what "they" say,
What is this thing being bandied about? What is "coping" anyway?
When viewed from the outside, looking in, it appears that I'm coping quite well.
No constant tears, I'm feeding myself and hiding the inner hell.

More tragedies and traumas come via internet and text,
The stomach-churning worry of the waiting for what's next.
The dregs of caring energy, an emergency reserve,
Were spent on those outside of me, – shredding a smarting nerve.
"Don't make yourself available, battered by bad news.
Switch it off! Protect yourself! It's a form of self-abuse!"

With more talking time to understand the processes inside,
There's a growing self-acceptance – I have no need to hide.
Weighing up what I've gone through before, the things that I have said,
I can see that I've been moving on, thoughts changing in my head.

If it seems that I won't get involved, that on the edge I stand,
It's because I'm totally committed to the job I have in hand.
An exhausting rebuilding programme is going on within,
Kept under wraps, as ideas gel, unfolding plans begin.

I'm as vulnerable as a hermit crab, seeking to change its shell,
But, reviewing all, I can now say, "I think I'm coping well!"

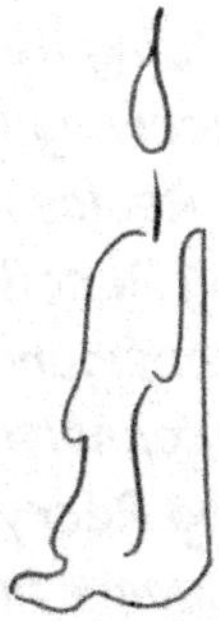

29 Re:Me

Reacting Realizing Reappraising Rearranging
Reassessing Reassuring Reattempting
Rebelling
Rebounding Rebuilding Rebuking Recalling
Receding Receiving Recharging
Reciting Reclaiming Reclassifying Recognizing
Recoiling Recollecting
Reconfiguring
Reconnecting Reconnoitring Recounting
Recovering Re-creating Recrystallizing Rectifying
Recuperating
Recurring Redefining Redressing Reducing
Re-emerging Re-enacting Re-entering
Re-evaluating
Re-examining Refining Refocusing Reforming
Re-forming Refraining Refreshing
Refusing
Refuting
Regarding Regathering Regenerating
Re-gilding
Regressing Regretting
Rehabilitating Reiterating Rejecting
Rejuvenating Rekindling
Relapsing

Relating Relaxing Relearning
Relenting
Reliving Relocating Remaining
Remedying Remembering
Remonstrating Renovating Re-opposing
Repairing Repatriating Repeating Repelling
Replenishing
Reposing
Repressing Reproaching Requesting
Re-scripting Researching Reselecting
Resenting
Resiling Resisting Resolving
Respecting Responding Restarting
Resting
Restoring
Restraining Restricting
Resurfacing Rethinking Retracing Retrieving
Returning
Reuniting
Revealing Reviewing Revising Revisiting
Reviving Revoking Revolving
Reworking Rewriting
Re-xraying
Re-me-ing

30 | Dormant

How could I have done it? Just left them to die!
Abandoned in the dark shed!
And then I discovered some more helpless ones,
struggling under the bed!

They'd arrived as a gift at Christmas time.
I was thrilled to receive them – and so,
I read the instructions and took it all in
and promised I'd help them to grow.

The box had a picture of beautiful blooms,
their petals lit up by the sun.
Inside was a pot, packs of bulbs and some soil
– this was going to be fun!

But left in the darkness, hermetically sealed,
the bulbs attempted to grow,
threw out spindly shoots as they searched for some light,
tissue ghost-flowers, with nowhere to go.

The bulb tried to flower, drained its store held within,
needing light, soil and warmth to thrive.
It needed to leave the dark, chilling place
or it would shrivel, no longer survive.

The good gardener knows each dormant bulb's need,
not forgetting them in the cold store,
and at the right time he carries them out,
to the warm soil and sunshine once more.

And I've been alone in a cold, dark place,
Taking those around me for granted.
But I think I'm now ready to dig myself in
and to blossom where I've been planted.

31 Driven

"What do you mean, you're chickening out?
You're quite capable of driving your car!
Why can't you do it again this weekend?
Last Tuesday you went twice as far!"

My thoughts fluctuate and waver so much.
Sometimes I feel I am ready
To step outside my comfort zone,
Then, at other times, I'm unsteady.

I am doing much more than I could before,
I've come so far this year.
I meet with friends, listen, talk and help,
Stepping forward, unhindered by fear.

But a little nudge and I'm teetering,
Off balance, out of kilter.
From dizzying heights of self-confidence,
I slide down a helter-skelter.

Is there a rhyme or reason for this?
Am I stretching myself too far?
Or is it the case, when exhaustion sets in,
That I need to lower the bar?

I will take a leaf out of the athlete's book,
When, after a gruelling event,
Recovery time is balanced against
The amount of energy spent.

It is hard to admit that, at times, I can't cope,
My compulsions challenge a duel,
But balance and strength come through meeting the need
To take time out, to rest and refuel.

32 Along the River

Here we go, a-dabbling along a gentle stream,
Here we go a-dabbling, our life is such a dream,
Love and Peace come to you,
And to you a-dabbling too,
And God bless you and send you a babbling little stream,
And God send you a peaceful, happy dream.

Here we go a-paddling, the water's getting rough,
Here we go a-paddling, we've nearly had enough!
Love and Peace come to you,
And to you strong paddling too,
And God bless you and send you his strength when it gets rough,
And God send you more strength when it gets tough.

Here we go a-panicking, the whirlpool spins us round,
Here we go a-panicking, we're going to be drowned!
Love and Peace come to you,
And to you, no fear too,
And God bless you and send you his peace as you spin round,
And God send you no fear of being drowned.

Here we go a-floating on the river as it flows,
Here we go a-floating calmly with it where it goes,
Love and Peace come to you,
And to you sweet comfort too,
And God bless you and send you calmly where the water flows,
And God send you floating where his river goes.

33 Diversions

Hurtling along the motorway, I speed from A to B,
Then screech to a halt – there's an accident!
The diversion signs I can see.

Should I stay where I am, in the traffic jam, hoping that things will improve?
Or take a route along unknown ways,
having courage to make a move?

Leaving the highway, down dark, winding lanes, I flee to retreat from the world.
Experience tells me more traumas will come,
so I hide, licking wounds, tightly curled.

A five year plan? You're having a laugh! Long-term planning gets hijacked, I've found.
I've been grabbed by the scruff, shaken up and put down,
now I'm facing the other way round!

I'll put dates in my diary and plan in advance for things that I'd like to do.
Or appointments to keep, if all goes to plan,
no guarantee that I'll follow it through.

"How will I be?" and "Who will I be?" – if I'm losing the life that I've known?
My life's in free-fall, I've got no plan at all.
I pray that I will be shown.

Solo hang-glider flight, toes curled over the edge, sick stomach clenched with fear.
Will the straps hold me tight? Will the sail catch the breeze?
Instructions I'll no longer hear!

I'm trusting the maker as I leap into space and plummet like a stone.
As rocks rush to meet me, I reset the sail
and remember all I've been shown.

I see below me the cliffs and the crags, as I soar on this eagle's wing.
I knew all the theory, had studied the map,
now I'm flying and my heart can sing!

I drift on the thermals, led by the breeze to a place where it's safe to land.
"You are here!" "Yes, I'm here!" A welcoming greeting.
I'm found! It's all been planned.

75

34 An Easter Candle

Sadness crept in over Easter time,
A loneliness smothering fun,
Overwhelmed by a Good Friday grief,
A shadow-time had begun.

Days of existing alone in the darkness,
Not knowing which way to turn,
Longing for the sorrow to lift,
For an Easter sunrise to burn.

Then peering across the grief-darkened valley,
Sight caught a pinprick of light,
Marking the way to a place called home,
A light left on in the night.

The smallest beam shone a way through the blackness
A glimmer of hope was born,
From deepest darkness burst the brightest light,
And night was the backdrop for dawn.

35 The Outcast

Anxiety said to Happiness
"Keep Out! You have no place here!
How could you think that you belong in the realm of *Pain* and *Fear!*"

"I'm the one in charge! I control this land!
I tell you, there's not a chance
of improving things, of any hope that you'll ever laugh or dance!"

So *Happiness* left, slid away out of sight,
a fragile, vulnerable wraith,
no match for the bully, *Anxiety*, she abandoned *Hope* and *Faith*.

But *Love* heard of the plight of *Happiness*,
brought *Faith* and *Hope* to bear
against the insidious allies of *Fear*, *Anxiety* and *Despair*.

And mighty *Love* flowed throughout the land,
Disarming *Fear* and *Pain*,
brought *Peace* and *Solace* to a fertile place where *Faith* and *Hope* could remain.

One day, in the distance, some strangers appeared,
cautious steps approaching the land.
Acceptance and *Thankfulness* had arrived, holding *Happiness* by the hand.

Then *Love* and *Faith* rose, ran towards them with *Hope*,
Peace embraced and led them in
and *Laughter* linked arms with *Happiness*, the dance was about to begin.

36 Hope Springs

Hey! Come out and see what I have found
Right here in the wintry garden!
What's that you're saying? Oh! "Shut the door!"
I'm sorry, I beg your pardon.

Yes, I know that you've been feeling rough,
You're still flat out on the settee.
Back to back Christmas movies are numbing the pain,
But this I want you to see!

You might need to wrap yourself up warm,
Pop on your new quilted coat.
Put that hat on your head- like a Christmas pud
And a scarf 'round your croaking throat.

So, just step outside for a moment or two
While the sun's out and there's some blue sky.
The robins are singing with joy, fit to burst!
Come on now! Please, give it a try!

Look! Here are some delicate primrose flowers.
Over there catkins dance on the tree.
The forget-me-nots and love-in-a-mist
Have seedlings. Can you see?

They've all been waiting since Autumn's end,
Hit by hail and the withering frost,
And when they were smothered by a blanket of snow
I feared that they had been lost.

Let's keep looking out to the garden each day
To find hope that sweet primroses bring
And, although it's still winter and more snow may fall,
They'll sing, "It'll soon be spring!"

37 Meadow Sweet

I'm heading towards the meadow,
The place where my true love dwells,
In the shade of a sapling oak tree,
Encircled by seas of bluebells.

To hear the breeze caressing the grass
And its whisper in the trees,
In harmony with the woodland birds,
And the humming of the bees.

To sit amongst the meadowsweet,
Where the blue forget-me-nots grow,
Remembering meadows where we have lain,
Where I can no longer go.

Butterflies dance in the woodland glade,
Common Blue and Marbled White,
As dry grasses wave in the summer breeze,
One's gone, now out of sight.

I'll come with a primrose posy,
In lady's smock I will lay,
Wild cherries, the floating confetti,
On our second wedding day.

He waits in a sunlit meadow,
No petals fade, fall to the ground,
We'll meet in the light, together again,
Where the source of our love is found.

38　Daughters of the Dawn

As darkness falls a wild thing calls,

all colour drains away.

Tusk, tooth and claw in the Feary Fog,

she clings to the threads of the day.

Lost and afraid, the Scaries loom large,

her truth is distorted by fear,

Fight, flight or freeze? She searches the wood,

brave voices she's longing to hear.

Scrambling up to the crux of a tree,

she peers down to a terror-filled mire.

A warrior voice speaks into her mind,

"Look up! Keep climbing,

still higher."

Dawning light shows her clearly the fort to the east,

surrounded by ramparts and ditches.

Her safe place re-found,

head-compass reset,

into the fog she pitches.

The Maiden stands bathed in the dawning light,

looks back to the valley below.

The Light-Giver breathes on the Feary Fog,

night-demons, sun-banished

must go.

Far away to the east, in a hot, barren land, a Gadarene daughter is led

to see torment and fear rack the man of the graves,

many demons controlling his head.

Authority's voice commands them to leave,

gives them no choice but to go.

Light dawns, Peace has come,

Fear leaves in the swine,

pouring over the cliff,

drowned below.

Day that dawns in the east, spreads to lands in the west.

Lost, dark worlds are flooded with light.

The Light-Giver leads through the thick, Feary Fog,

lighting the way,

giving sight.

Two thousand years later, she walks through the woods,

       tears streaming from heartache and strife.

Sight fixed on the ground, her hope is decaying,

       her lover's not long for this life.

Her eyes, dim with grief, see through thicket and thorns,

       to a sapling, cut off in its prime.

Its branches, flung out form the arms of a cross,

       peace-symbol for her through this time.

Leaving Night in the Forest, the Maid travelled west,

       seeing tracks where past footsteps had been.

Passing the Maiden, high on her hill,

       to the fog and the cliffs not yet seen.

The grieving Maid, on a western coast,

                seeks rest in the Lee of a hill,

stumbling her way through the Valley of Death,

                    exhausted,

                her thoughts never still.

Of a daughter in darkness, a story is told.

                No peace for her, where could she go?

Lost and tormented, jilted love leaps,

                  hope dashed

                on the sharp rocks below.

But the Maid climbs on upwards, a zig-zagging path,

                resting, admiring the scene.

Looks back down through trees to the dread-darkened valley,

                now seeing where she has been.

She's on the right path as the mist slowly clears.

                "Keep climbing," she hears a voice say,

"Your foot will not slip, mighty warriors are guarding,

                Light-Giver is leading the way."

So, climbing on up to the strong lookout tower,

                her foot is quite firm, she's not fazing.

There a cross rises high, against blazing blue sky,

                the view from the top is amazing.

As the Maiden lies sleeping, a different day dawns,

a drone rises up with the sun.

Its images beamed through blue sky and ether,

humanity linked – every one.

As it flew high above ancient valleys and cliffs,

the Maid silently watching in awe,

The Light-Giver breathed, banished fog to the sea,

pouring over the cliff,

gone once more.

Millennials' mother, she looks back to Before,

sees the Daughters and Maidens again,

Knows their fears and their hopes, their courage and faith,

the threads of their days still remain.

A Daughter of Light, with no fear of the darkness,

an LED torch in her hand,

Linked to the world, linked through time,

linked by dawnings,

she's led

by The Light

through the land.

39 You Are The One

You are the one who sits beside me
In the ashes of my grief,
Patiently, not urging action,
While I lie beyond belief.

You are the one with words of comfort,
Water in a desert land.
As I drink in what is offered
Hope springs up through lifeless sand.

You are the one who waits beside me
As I stretch my aching heart,
Atrophied through years of grieving,
Loving growth can gently start.

You are the one who's there beside me
Through the setbacks and the pain,
Giving me fresh strength and courage
As I learn to walk again.

You are the one who walks beside me,
Taking your hand it's then I know,
Together, onward, ever upwards,
This is the moment, now, "Let's Go!"

Found

I am thankful to God for sending Jesus – The Light of the World,
who shines into the darkest places,
offering forgiveness, peace, security and love.
We are never alone.

I am also thankful to have found light through
special people, places and things that have touched my life,
- candles illuminating the path.